# SPARK ISLAND

## KS2 Skills Practice
## MATHS
## Learning Adventures

**Simon Greaves and Helen Greaves**

# Introduction

## About this book

Maths affects our everyday lives and like the Elders of Sparkopolis, who have taken ten years to design and build their wonderful city, we need to understand and use mathematical skills to solve problems. So why not join The Gang to find out more about Maths and how exciting it can be!

## How to use this book

Think about the best time for using this book. It might be easier at a weekend or early in the evening. Most of all, pick a quiet time when your child is eager to learn and not too tired. Find a suitable place where he or she can work comfortably without being disturbed, then make a start on one of the activities.

Your child may prefer to work through the book page by page, or alternatively you could suggest activities that you feel will be more useful. Whichever approach you adopt, try to make it an enjoyable and positive experience for your child. Discuss the activities together and give lots of praise and encouragement along the way. All the answers are at the back of the book for quick and easy checking!

## How you can help

- Remember little and often is best! Children's brains can only take so much, it's best to stop before they get bored and grumpy.
- You can help your child by reading questions, testing knowledge of facts, marking answers and discussing topics that your child finds difficult.
- Use the *Spark Island KS2 National Tests Maths* for some more exciting activities, or log on to the Spark Island website (www.sparkisland.com) for your child to take part in some interactive fun.
- Most of all, encourage your child, praise his or her efforts and use the gold stickers to reward good work.

# Contents

# Numbers and the number system

The Elders are planning to introduce a new number system into Spark Island. They have been investigating our number system and the way it works.

**1** Here are some 3-digit numbers which look the same upside down.

**III**     **609**     **8I8**

Find all the other 3-digit numbers that have this special quality.

**2** If 60 S in a M stands for 60 **seconds** in a **minute**, help the Elders work out what each of these means.

| 24 H in a D | 29 D in F in a L Y |
|---|---|
| 24 Hours in a D | 29 |

| 11 P in a F T | 7 W of the W |
|---|---|

**3** The Elders have also been studying the Roman method of numbering. The Romans used capital letters to represent the numbers 1, 5, 10, 50,100, 500 and 1000.

Write these numbers in Roman numerals.

7 VII     16 XVI     34 XXXIV     67 _____

101 _____     630 _____     1254 _____

## Roman numerals

| 1 I | 5 V |
|---|---|
| 10 X | 50 L |
| 100 C | 500 D |
| 1000 M | |

Other numbers are made by combining these letters.

Examples:

| 3 | III | (1 + 1 + 1) |
|---|---|---|
| 4 | IV | (5 – 1) |
| 6 | VI | (5 + 1) |
| 15 | XV | (10 + 5) |
| 32 | XXXII | (10 + 10 + 10 + 1 + 1) |
| 41 | XLI | (50 – 10 + 1) |
| 205 | CCV | (100 + 100 + 5) |

Put these numbers in order from smallest to largest to spell out the name of one of Sparkopolis' inhabitants.

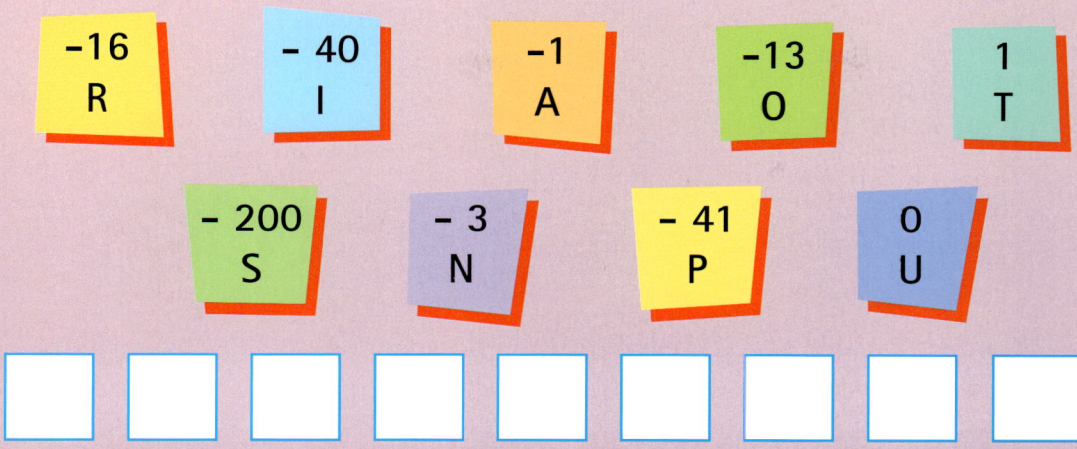

| –16 R | – 40 I | –1 A | –13 O | 1 T |
|---|---|---|---|---|

| – 200 S | – 3 N | – 41 P | 0 U |
|---|---|---|---|

☐ ☐ ☐ ☐ ☐ ☐ ☐ ☐ ☐

**5** Shade in the letter next to the **smaller** number in each pair.  Example:  1·7 A    1·6 B

Now you try.

| 0·63 | J | 0·36 | P |
|---|---|---|---|
| 0·04 | O | 0·4 | E |
| 1·61 | L | 1·67 | T |
| 4·3 | P | 3·4 | K |
| 0·02 | S | 0·12 | A |
| 3·62 | C | 3·26 | T |
| 5·0 | K | 0·5 | E |

The letters that you have not shaded spell out an essential item for one of Sparkopolis' residents.

☐

## Back and forth

This is a game for two players.

**You will need** two counters, two 1-6 dice and some sticky labels.

Cut out twelve small squares from the sticky labels and cover each number on the two dice.

On one dice write the numbers: -4, -2, -1, 1, 3, 5.

On the second dice write the numbers: -4, -3, -2, 2, 3, 5.

Place the two counters on the START ZONE on the game board. Take turns to roll both dice and add the two numbers together.

If your total is negative, move backwards that number.

Example:  dice show -4 and -2
your total is -6
move backwards 6 spaces.

If your total is positive, move forwards that number.

Example:  dice show -1 and 3
your total is 2
move forwards 2 spaces.

The game ends when one player reaches either END ZONE.
You must roll the exact total to land on the END ZONE.

### Zeb's fact file

A million is 1 000 000 (six zeros).

A billion is 1 000 000 000 (nine zeros).

A trillion is 1 000 000 000 000 (twelve zeros).

A googol has one hundred zeros!

### FIND OUT
Find out how many things there are in:

a brace _____    a score _____

a dozen _____    a gross _____

### DID YOU KNOW?
The lowest temperature ever recorded was a very chilly −89°C at Vostok in Antarctica on 21 July 1983.

17 18 19 20 **END ZONE**

16
15

14 13 12 11
10
9

5 6 7 8
4
3

2 1 **START ZONE** -1 -2
-3
-4

-8 -7 -6 -5
-9
-10

-11 -12 -13 -14
-15
-16

**END ZONE** -20 -19 -18 -17

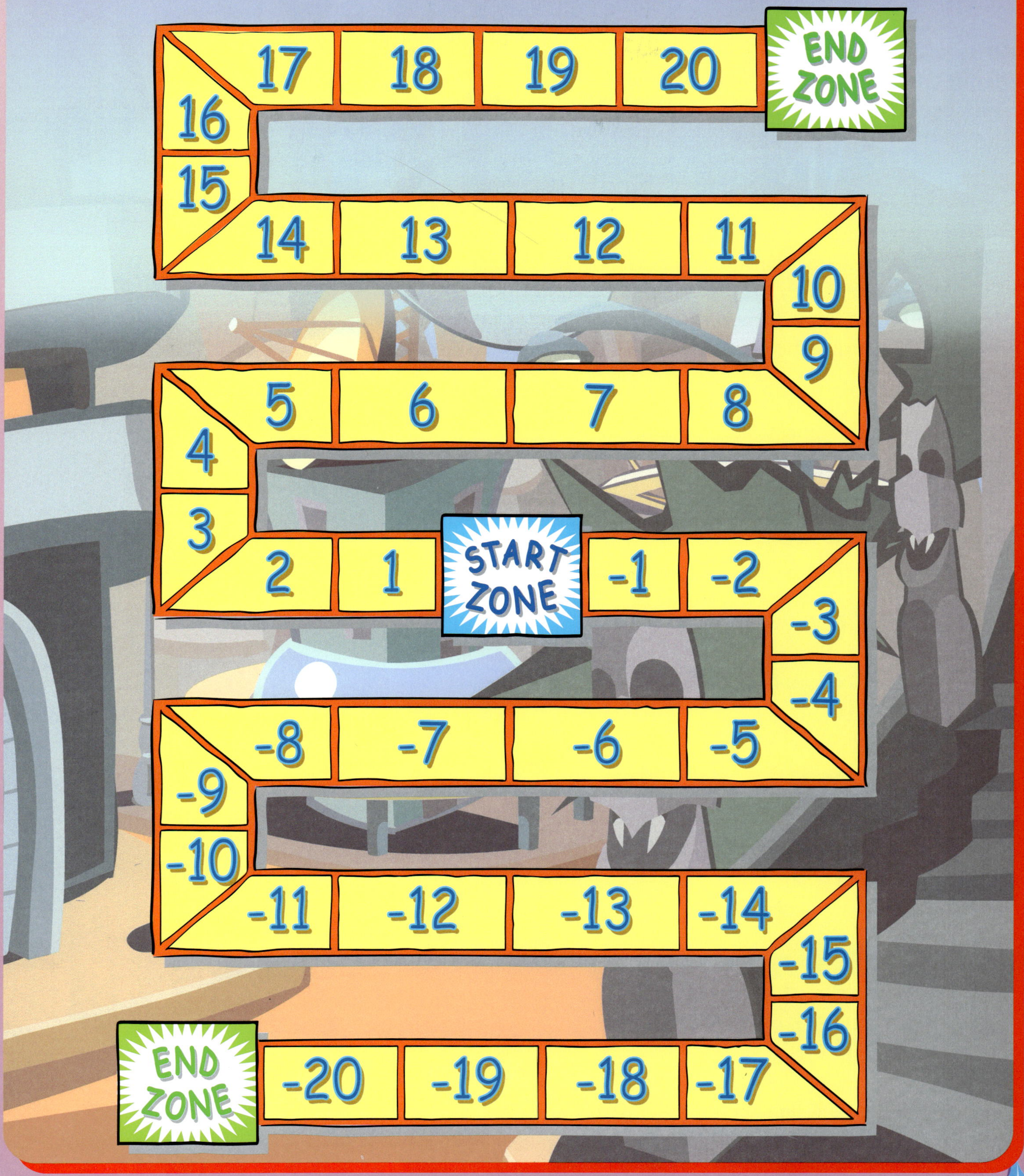

# Calculations

It is several weeks since the Gang escaped from Grunge Hall and, since then, they have not been to school. Zeb decides it's time for some maths lessons.

**1** Xybok just love eating raspberries but they hate them when they are too ripe. To pass the time they have been throwing over-ripe raspberries at the targets below.

Each raspberry that hits the outer ring scores double.

The centre scores 50.

Work out the total scores for each target.

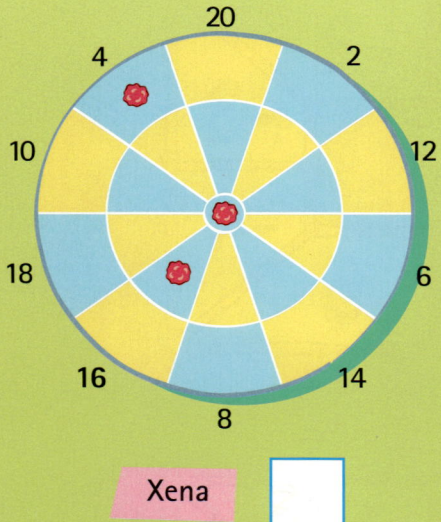

Xena ☐

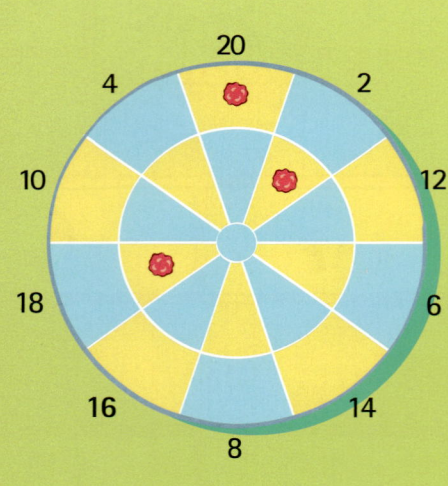

Xak ☐

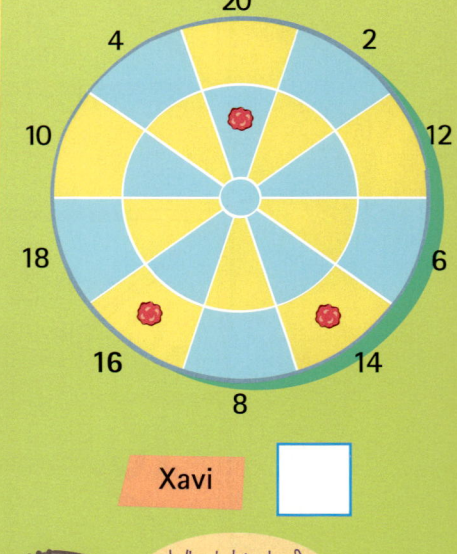

Xavi ☐

Which Xybok has scored the most? ☐

What kind of pliers do you use in maths?

Multipliers.

**2** These digits can be used to make numbers.

7  9  1  3  4  4

(a) Make two 3-digit numbers which, when added together, have the highest total.

☐☐☐  ☐☐☐

(b) Now make two 3-digit numbers which, when added together, have the lowest total.

☐☐☐  ☐☐☐

(c) Finally, make three 2-digit numbers with the highest total.

☐☐  ☐☐  ☐☐

Why was six scared?

Because seven eight nine.

**3** Draw a single straight line to divide the square into two sections so that the total in each section is 1·8.

| | | |
|---|---|---|
| 0·4 | 0·3 | |
| 0·5 | 0·5 | 0·3 |
| 0·1 | 0·4 | 0·6 |
| 0·3 | 0·2 | |

**4** Using all the digits below and some of the four rules of number Zeb has made the answer 614.

50  2  5  9  6

This is how I did it.

$2 \times 6 = 12$

$12 \times 50 = 600$

$600 + 5 + 9 = 614$

Can you make the answer 263 using all the same digits and any of the four rules.

**5** Many numbers can be written as a sum of two or more consecutive numbers, but some cannot.

(a) Find consecutive numbers which give the totals in the table. Two have been done for you and five cannot be done.

| | | | |
|---|---|---|---|
| | = 1 | | = 11 |
| | = 2 | | = 12 |
| | = 3 | | = 13 |
| | = 4 | | = 14 |
| | = 5 | 7 + 8 | = 15 |
| | = 6 | | = 16 |
| | = 7 | | = 17 |
| | = 8 | | = 18 |
| | = 9 | | = 19 |
| | = 10 | 2 + 3 + 4 + 5 + 6 | = 20 |

(b) Which five totals cannot be made?
Do you notice anything special about these numbers?

| | | | | |
|---|---|---|---|---|
| | | | | |

**6** Fit the numbers 1 to 16 into the square so that the total of each row, column and diagonal is the same. Some numbers have already been done for you.

| 16 | 3 | | |
|---|---|---|---|
| | | 10 | | 8 |
| 9 | | 7 | |
| | 15 | 14 | 1 |

**Numbers to words**

Do these calculations on your calculator then turn it upside down and read the words.

1. 904 x 904 + 89621818
   (clue – a prickly creature)

2. 230 x 230·5 + 30
   (clue – Spydrax favourites)

3. 50·19 – (5 x 0·0039)
   (clue – not liquids or gases)

**7** Here are some special offers from the Sparkopolis Shoe Shop.

**Spark Island Shoes**

Streetfeet 2 — £65.50

Streetfeet 2ZX — £78.30

Spydrax boots SETS OF 6 — £42.00

Spydrax sandals SETS OF 6 — £28.80

(a) The Spydrax shoes are sold in sets of six.
Stan Spydrax has lost one of his new sandals.
He wants to buy one to replace it.

How much does one sandal cost?

(b) Strat is going to buy a new pair of trainers.
He can't decide between Streetfeet 2 and Streetfeet 2ZX.

What is the difference between the prices?

# Properties of numbers and sequences

**1** When the Gang first arrived in Sparkopolis the streets seemed like a maze but then Zeb found a quick way of getting to the Library. He found a route which follows only multiples of 9.

Draw Zeb's route on the maze.

**2** Circle the number which is not prime.

| 17 | 7 | 11 | 15 | 2 | 3 |
|----|---|----|----|---|---|

**3** Prime numbers can be **added** together to make other numbers.

**(a)** Find prime numbers to complete these calculations.

$\boxed{6} + \boxed{6} = 12$     $\boxed{\phantom{0}} + \boxed{\phantom{0}} = 25$

$\boxed{8} + \boxed{8} = 16$     $\boxed{\phantom{0}} + \boxed{\phantom{0}} + \boxed{\phantom{0}} = 21$

**(b)** Prime numbers can be **multiplied** together to make other numbers. Find prime numbers to complete these multiplications.

$\boxed{\phantom{0}} \times \boxed{\phantom{0}} = 15$     $\boxed{\phantom{0}} \times \boxed{\phantom{0}} = 55$

$\boxed{\phantom{0}} \times \boxed{\phantom{0}} = 26$     $\boxed{\phantom{0}} \times \boxed{\phantom{0}} \times \boxed{\phantom{0}} = 30$

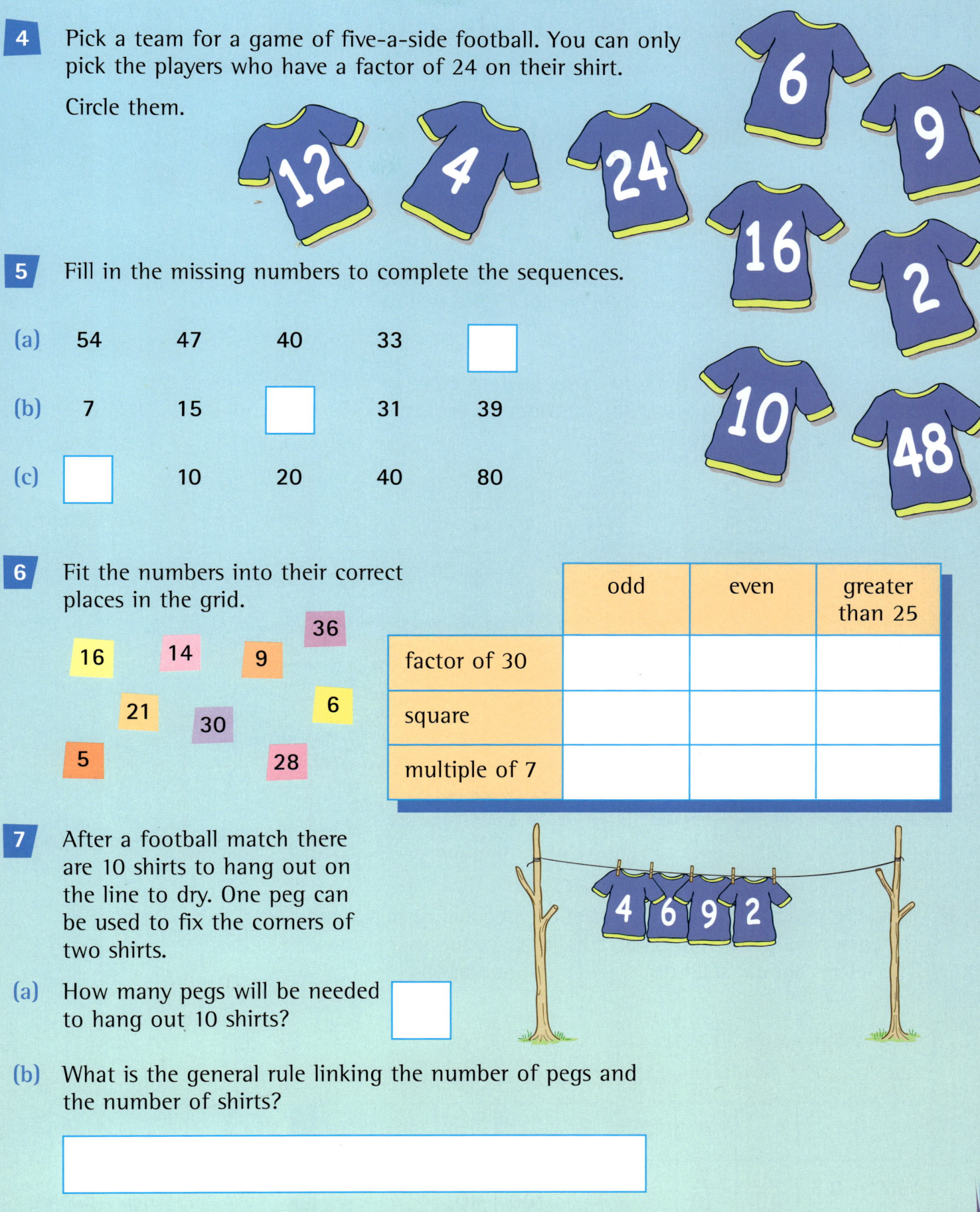

**4** Pick a team for a game of five-a-side football. You can only pick the players who have a factor of 24 on their shirt.

Circle them.

**12  4  24  6  9  16  2  10  48**

**5** Fill in the missing numbers to complete the sequences.

(a)  54    47    40    33    ☐

(b)  7    15    ☐    31    39

(c)  ☐    10    20    40    80

**6** Fit the numbers into their correct places in the grid.

16  14  9  36  21  30  6  5  28

|  | odd | even | greater than 25 |
|---|---|---|---|
| factor of 30 |  |  |  |
| square |  |  |  |
| multiple of 7 |  |  |  |

**7** After a football match there are 10 shirts to hang out on the line to dry. One peg can be used to fix the corners of two shirts.

(a) How many pegs will be needed to hang out 10 shirts?  ☐

(b) What is the general rule linking the number of pegs and the number of shirts?

☐

# Fractions, decimals and percentages

Dotty planted eight tulip bulbs in a pot. When they flowered she found that out of the eight, four were red, two were yellow and two were white.

That means $\dfrac{4}{8} = \dfrac{1}{2} = 50\% = 0.5$ are red.

$\dfrac{2}{8} = \dfrac{1}{4} = 25\% = 0.25$ are yellow or white.

**1**  Copy these equivalent fraction cards on to a piece of card and cut them out. Arrange them in a loop so that the fraction on the end of one card matches that on another.

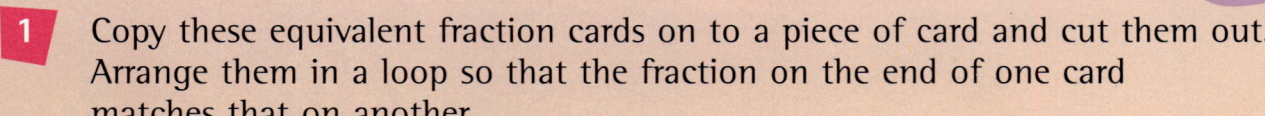

| $\dfrac{1}{2}$ | $\dfrac{2}{5}$ | $\dfrac{3}{8}$ | $\dfrac{1}{4}$ | $\dfrac{5}{8}$ | $\dfrac{9}{15}$ |
|---|---|---|---|---|---|
| $\dfrac{4}{12}$ | $\dfrac{8}{12}$ | $\dfrac{10}{16}$ | $\dfrac{4}{10}$ | $\dfrac{10}{80}$ | $\dfrac{2}{3}$ |

| $\dfrac{4}{5}$ | $\dfrac{3}{4}$ | $\dfrac{6}{8}$ | $\dfrac{9}{24}$ | $\dfrac{3}{5}$ | $\dfrac{3}{12}$ |
|---|---|---|---|---|---|
| $\dfrac{4}{20}$ | $\dfrac{8}{10}$ | $\dfrac{1}{8}$ | $\dfrac{1}{3}$ | $\dfrac{2}{4}$ | $\dfrac{1}{5}$ |

**2**  Find the matching equivalent fraction, decimal or percentage for each one in the table. Write its letter in the space provided. The letters should spell out a place in Sparkopolis.

P 3%   R 0.75   L $\dfrac{3}{10}$   K 25%   A 0.1   C 0.7   D 50%   B 0.55   S $\dfrac{1}{5}$   O 0.05

| | | | | | | | | | | | | | |
|---|---|---|---|---|---|---|---|---|---|---|---|---|---|
| 55% | 0.3 | $\dfrac{1}{10}$ | $\dfrac{7}{10}$ | $\dfrac{1}{4}$ | 20% | $\dfrac{3}{100}$ | $\dfrac{1}{10}$ | 75% | $\dfrac{1}{4}$ | 75% | 5% | $\dfrac{1}{10}$ | 0.5 |

**3** The Gang have been racing each other over a distance of 100 m.

**(a)** One of the Elders has timed them. Here are the race results.
Round each of the Gang's times to the nearest second and then
the nearest tenth of a second. Fill in the table.

| Name | Time (seconds) | Time rounded to nearest second | Time rounded to nearest tenth of a second |
|------|------|------|------|
| Dotty | 21·23 | 2o | |
| Milo | 24·76 | 8 o | |
| Zeb | 20·88 | | |
| Nina | 18·12 | | |
| Strat | 17·45 | | |

**(b)** Fill in the medals with the names of the Gang who took first, second and third place.

1st place — Strat

2nd place — Nina

3rd place — Zeb

**(c)** What is the difference between the fastest time and the slowest time?

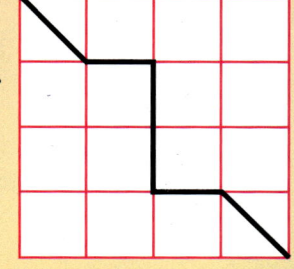 seconds

$$\begin{array}{r} 24\cdot76 \\ -\ 17\cdot45 \\ \hline 07\cdot31 \end{array}$$

**4** The square has been divided into two halves.

Find four other different ways to divide the square in half.

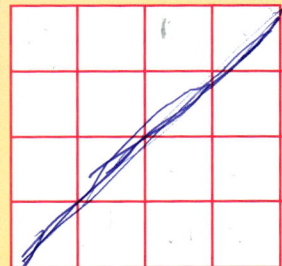
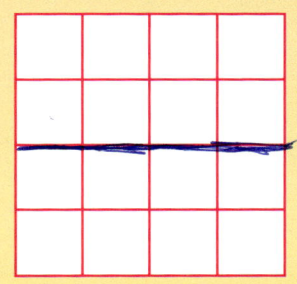
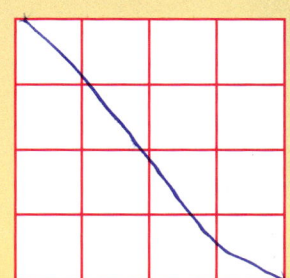
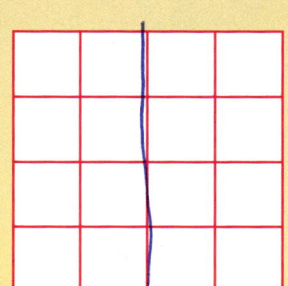

**5** Zeb has a huge bar of chocolate. Milo has asked him for some pieces of it. Zeb gives Milo a choice. He can either have 20 pieces or 20% of the bar.

(a) Colour in these two options on the bars below.

Which would you choose? 

(b) What fraction of the whole bar is 20 squares? 

(c) What fraction of the bar is 20%? 

## A whole fraction

One half, two eighths and a quarter
Wanted to start up a fight,
They fought and hit each other
With all their number might.

They then decided to make up
As unity was their goal,
'Cos one half, two eighths and a quarter
Always make a whole.

**Yesterday I heard a joke about decimals but I didn't get the point.**

**Fractions speak louder than words.**

### Zeb's fact file

In the UK, just over 51% of the population are female and just under 49% are male.

**6** Labels on packets of food show us information about the content of the food inside. A label usually shows how much of each food type it contains **per 100 grams.** This means it's easy to work out the **percentage** of each food type.

| Bran Cereal | per 100 grams |
|---|---|
| Protein | 11·8 grams |
| Carbohydrate | 52·3 grams |
| Fat | 4·7 grams |
| Fibre | 3·3 grams |

4·7% of this cereal is fat.

**(a)** Find some food labels in your home and make a list of the items and the percentage of fat each contains.
Put them in order of the percentage of fat contained.

| Food | % Fat |
|---|---|
|  |  |
|  |  |
|  |  |
|  |  |
|  |  |

**REMINDER**

$\frac{1}{2}$ = 50% = 0·5

$\frac{1}{4}$ = 25% = 0·25

$\frac{3}{4}$ = 75% = 0·75

$\frac{1}{10}$ = 10% = 0·1

$\frac{1}{100}$ = 1% = 0·01

$\frac{1}{5}$ = 20% = 0·2

Which is the greater king — Henry III or Henry the VI?

Henry III of course.

Why?

Because one third is equal to two sixths!

# Ratio and proportion

**1** The Gang are preparing a party for Milo. Dotty is making Milo's favourite shortbread biscuits. She doesn't know the actual amounts to use but she can remember that the ratio of **sugar** to **butter** to **plain flour** is **1:2:3**.

(a) Why don't you try her recipe?

Start with 50 grams of sugar. How much butter and flour will you need using Dotty's ratio?

| butter: | grams |
| flour: | grams |

(b) Now follow these instructions. Make sure you ask an adult to help you.

> Mix the flour and sugar together in a bowl.
> Rub in the butter until it makes a mixture of fine crumbs.
> Knead the mixture to form a solid ball.
> Roll out the mixture until it is 1 cm thick.
> Cut out shapes using pastry cutters.
> Place on a greased baking sheet and bake for 15 minutes at 190°C.

**2** Strat is in charge of making the drinks. Here are the recipes he is using.

**Orange Sparkle**
Mix 2 measures of orange juice to 3 measures of lemonade.

**Raspberry Milk Shake**
Mix 1 part raspberry syrup to 7 parts ice cold milk.

(a) Strat uses 400 ml of orange juice. How much lemonade will he need?

(b) How much Orange Sparkle does he make?

(c) Strat wants to make 1 litre (1000 ml) of Raspberry Milk Shake. How much syrup and milk will he need?

**3** Nina has made some small cakes and put them on a tray. She needs to ice them with different coloured icing. Zeb, showing off his knowledge of proportion, asks her to ice the cakes as follows:

$\frac{1}{4}$ yellow, $\frac{1}{3}$ green, $\frac{3}{24}$ pink and the rest blue.

Use Zeb's instructions to colour the cakes below.

**4** Draw lines to join the equivalent ratios.

4:16

3:2

15:10        5:10

2:1

1:1

8:4

1:4

16:16

1:2

### Zeb's fact file

The ratio of the height of a man to the Eiffel Tower is 1:167.

The ratio of the height of a man to the Empire State Building is 1:212.

**REMINDER**
A ratio compares one part with another.
A proportion compares an amount to the whole.

# Handling data

The Phliplids are fascinated by Spark Island, its life-forms and the environment. They spend hours simply observing, taking notes and collecting data.

**1**  Charts, such as pie charts, bar charts and line graphs are used in everyday life to display data. You see them in magazines, newspapers and on TV.

Find some examples, cut them out and make a display.

What is a mathematician's favourite animal?

**2**  The Phliplids are recording the daily temperature on Spark Island.

You could record the temperature each day where you live. If you have a thermometer, place it outside and record the temperature in degrees Centigrade at the same time each day. If you don't have a thermometer you can find out temperatures from newspapers, TV weather forecasts or the internet.

A grrraph.

Plot your readings on the chart below. Join up the points to make a line graph.

**3** Find the words listed below in the grid. The words may be listed horizontally, vertically or diagonally.

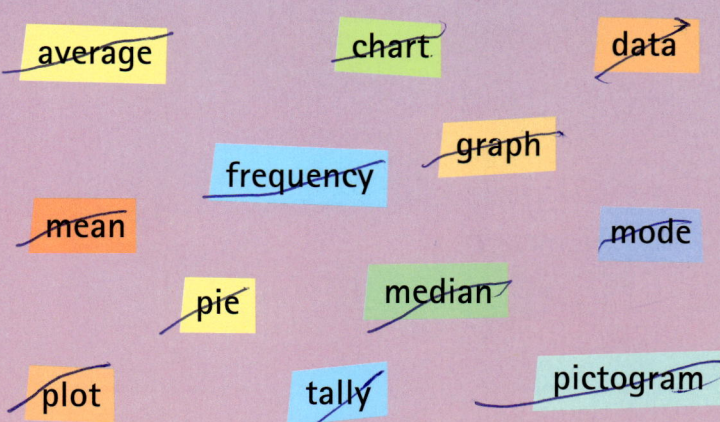

average
chart
data
graph
frequency
mean
mode
pie
median
plot
tally
pictogram

| f | h | a | j | f | t | b | a | t | j |
|---|---|---|---|---|---|---|---|---|---|
| w | r | v | z | l | c | h | a | r | t |
| s | n | e | p | h | m | t | g | l | k |
| t | a | r | q | e | o | e | r | l | i |
| a | i | a | d | u | d | r | a | o | e |
| l | d | g | r | a | e | q | p | n | v |
| l | e | e | t | x | t | n | h | s | c |
| y | m | a | r | g | o | t | c | i | p |
| s | d | f | d | g | l | g | w | y | f |
| a | e | i | p | h | p | k | t | a | s |

**4** Milo has bought a packet of sweets. His favourites are the orange ones but he's convinced that they put fewer orange sweets in the packet than any other colour.

**(a)** Test Milo's theory with your own packet of coloured sweets, such as fruit gums or jelly beans.

On the tally chart, first list the different colours of sweets in your packet. Then complete the tally chart and write down the frequency of each colour.

| Colour | Tally | Frequency |
|--------|-------|-----------|
|        |       |           |

**(b)** Use your results to complete the bar chart.

**(c)** Which is the modal colour?

**(d)** Is Milo's theory correct? Circle Yes or No.

Yes / No

Colour of sweet

**5** One of the Phliplids has been asked by the Spironauts to improve the design of their jetpacks. To help with his calculations, the Phliplid wants to find the mean weight of a Spironaut. He has weighed each one.

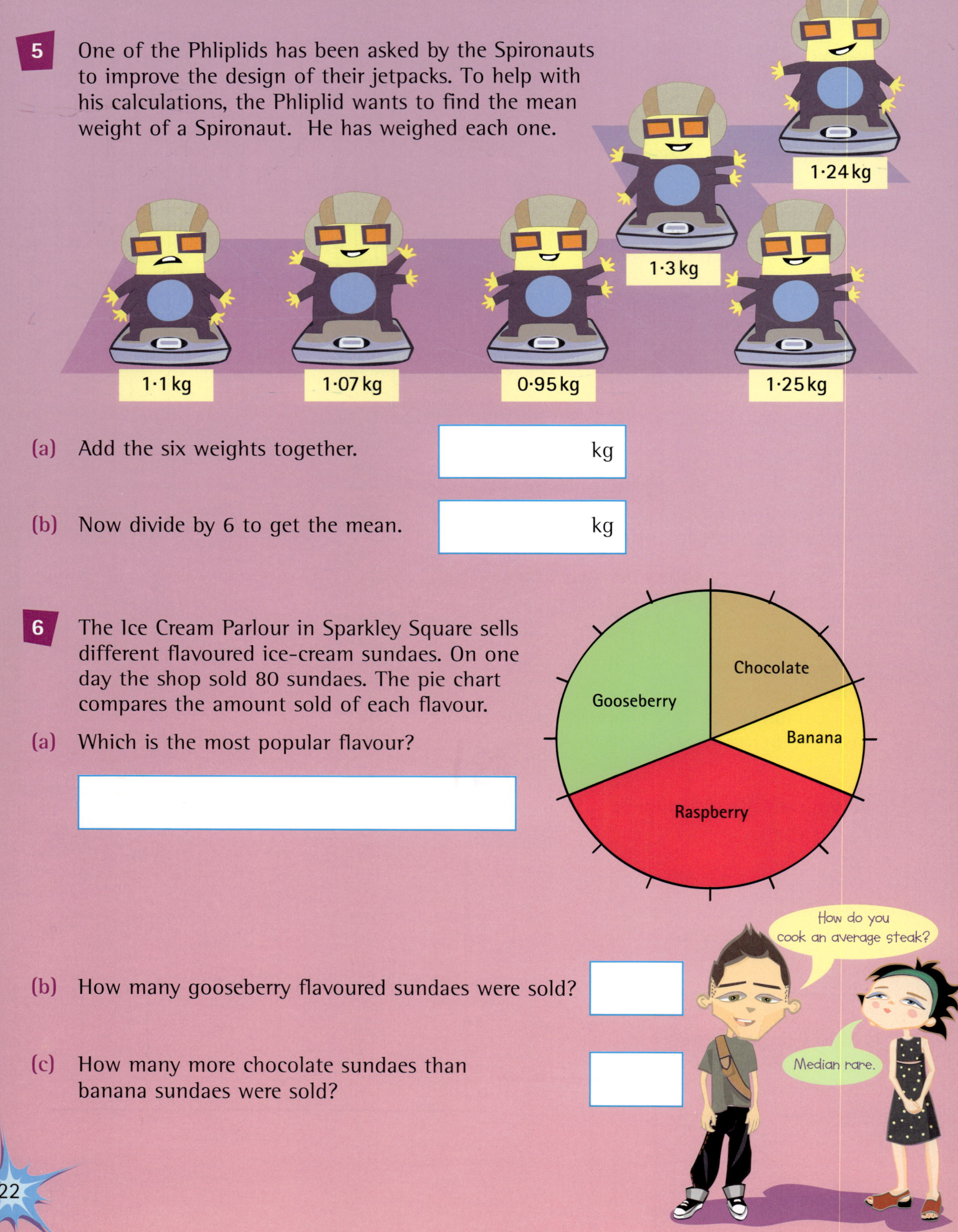

1·24 kg

1·3 kg

1·1 kg     1·07 kg     0·95 kg     1·25 kg

(a) Add the six weights together.          [ ] kg

(b) Now divide by 6 to get the mean.       [ ] kg

**6** The Ice Cream Parlour in Sparkley Square sells different flavoured ice-cream sundaes. On one day the shop sold 80 sundaes. The pie chart compares the amount sold of each flavour.

(a) Which is the most popular flavour?

[ ]

Chocolate

Gooseberry

Banana

Raspberry

How do you cook an average steak?

Median rare.

(b) How many gooseberry flavoured sundaes were sold?   [ ]

(c) How many more chocolate sundaes than banana sundaes were sold?   [ ]

**7** The table below contains information about some countries in the world.

| Country | Capital city | Continent | Population (millions) | Official language | Currency |
|---------|--------------|-----------|-----------------------|-------------------|----------|
| France | Paris | Europe | 60 | French | euro |
| USA | Washington DC | Americas | 281 | English | US dollar |
| Australia | Canberra | Australasia | 20 | English | Australian dollar |
| Spain | Madrid | Europe | 40 | Spanish | euro |
| Brazil | Brasilia | Americas | 176 | Portuguese | real |
| Japan | Tokyo | Asia | 127 | Japanese | yen |
| Nigeria | Abuja | Africa | 130 | English | naira |

(a) Which country has the capital city Brasilia?

(b) What is the population of the USA?

(c) Which countries are in Europe?

(d) How many countries have English as the official language?

(e) What is the currency of Nigeria?

**REMINDER**

In a list of numbers:

the **mode** is the most common item or number

the **median** is the middle number when listed in order of size

the **mean** is found by adding up all of the values and dividing by the number of values

the **range** is the difference between the largest and smallest numbers

**Mean and Mode**

Said mean to mode,
'You haven't a clue

'cos most often things are down to you'.

'You're average mean,' cried mode, 'and that you cannot fiddle.'

'I'd rather be this mean than like median in the middle.'

# Probability

**1** Zeb and Nina are playing the board game Sparkopoly.
They are using 2 dice each numbered 1 to 6.

Nina thinks that there is the same chance of scoring any total from 2 to 12.

Zeb thinks that it is more likely to score a total of 7 than any other total.
He has drawn this table to prove his point.

|   | 1 | 2 | 3 | 4 | 5 | 6 |
|---|---|---|---|---|---|---|
| 1 | 2 | 3 | 4 | 5 | 6 | 7 |
| 2 | 3 | 4 | 5 | 6 | 7 | 8 |
| 3 | 4 | 5 | 6 | 7 | 8 | 9 |
| 4 | 5 | 6 | 7 | 8 | 9 | 10 |
| 5 | 6 | 7 | 8 | 9 | 10 | 11 |
| 6 | 7 | 8 | 9 | 10 | 11 | 12 |

There are 36 different combinations.

There are six different ways to score a total of 7, more ways than for any other total.

The **probability** of scoring 7 is therefore $\frac{6}{36}$ or $\frac{1}{6}$.

**FINDING PROBABILITY**

Using fractions is the key
To finding probability.
Toss a coin or spin a spinner,
Guess it right and you're a winner!

(a) Which totals are least likely?

(b) How many different ways can you score 10?

(c) What is the probability of scoring 10?

24

**2** Nina has made her own board game and called it Take-a-Chance.
She has made some spinners with numbers 1, 2 and 3 on them.
Now she wants to choose a spinner which has a greater chance
of landing on 3 than 1 or 2.

Which of the five spinners should she choose?

Explain why

A

B

C

D

E

## How to play Take-a-Chance

This is a game for two players.

**You will need** one dice, one coin and two counters for the board game.

You will also need to make two spinners as shown below.
Copy these on to cardboard and push a pencil or used matchstick
through the centres so that they will spin.

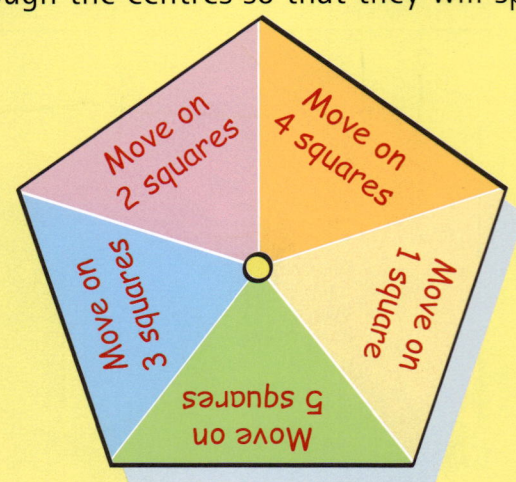

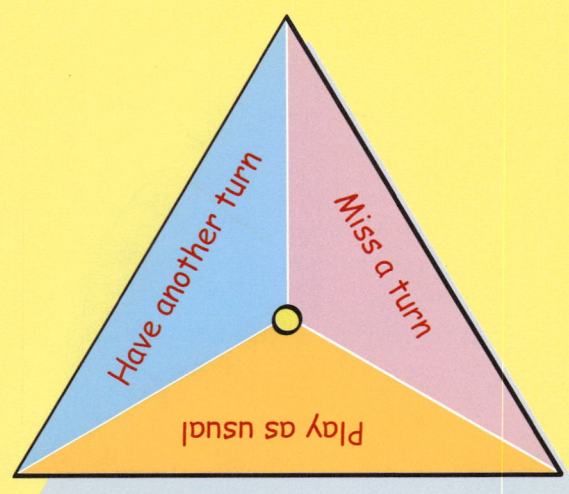

The rules of the game are as follows:

1  Place both counters at the start.

2  Take turns to roll the dice and move your counter
   forward for that number of squares.

3  If you land on a 'pentagon', 'triangle' or 'coin' square
   then either toss the coin or spin the appropriate spinner.

4  There are other squares with instructions. Be sure to
   follow them. You may be able to take a short cut.

5  The first player to get to the 'Win' square is the winner.

 spin this spinner

 spin this spinner

 toss the coin
- heads, move on 2
- tails, go back 2

What do you call a broken quadrilateral?

A rectangle!

### Zeb's fact file

The probability of being struck by lightning is believed to be about

$$\frac{1}{5\ 000\ 000}$$  (1 in 5 million).

The probability of winning the Lottery is about

$$\frac{1}{14\ 000\ 000}$$  (1 in 14 million).

# 2D shapes

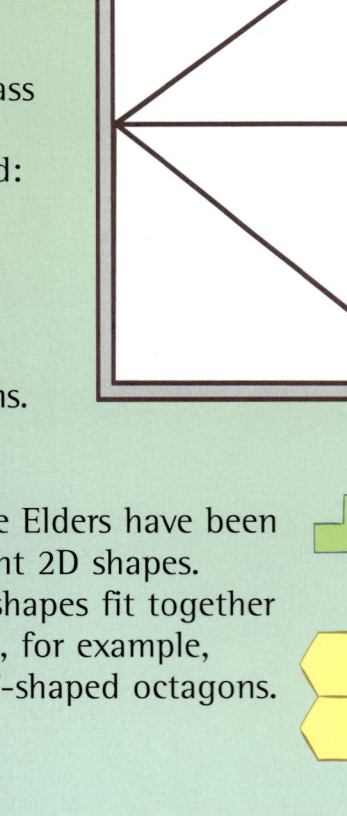

**1** The Elders are busy designing another new library for Sparkopolis.

One of the Elders has designed a stained glass window for the grand entrance hall. He has left instructions on how it should be painted: blue square, red trapezium, yellow kite, green parallelogram, orange pentagon, purple obtuse-angled triangle, all other shapes clear.

Colour the window following the instructions.

**2** The library is to have a lavish tiled floor. The Elders have been investigating the patterns formed by different 2D shapes. One of the Elders has found that some 2D shapes fit together to form a pattern, without leaving any gaps, for example, parallelograms, regular hexagons, irregular T-shaped octagons. These patterns are called **tessellations**.

**(a)** Find some other 2D shapes which tessellate.

**(b)** The Elders have found that more interesting patterns can be made by altering a simple shape which tessellates, such as a square.

Try this idea.

**1** Draw a square.

**2** Cut out a notch and position it on the opposite side. Do the same for the other pair of opposite sides.

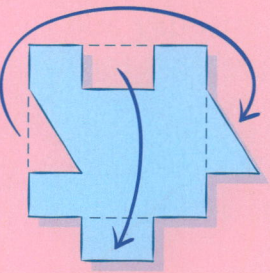

**3** Copy your 'tile' on to card and cut it out.

**4** Draw around it to create a pattern.

**5** Have another go but start with a different basic shape such as a hexagon.

**3** The Elders have noticed that their designs for the new library include many different 2D shapes.

Have a look around your home or your street to see how many you can find. Look for block paving, wallpaper, tiles, coins, kitchenware, furniture.

Make a list or, if you have a camera, you could take some pictures.

**What am I?**
I have four sides.
I have two pairs of equal sides.
I do not have any parallel sides.
I have one line of symmetry.
What am I?

| Object | Number of sides | Shape |
|---|---|---|
| 50 pence coin | 7 | heptagon |
|  |  |  |
|  |  |  |
|  |  |  |
|  |  |  |

# 3D shapes

**1** It's Nina's birthday and the rest of the Gang are wrapping presents for her.

They have wrapped six gifts. Each gift is a different 3D shape. Which shape is the odd one out? Draw a ring around it.

**2** Try this really useful way of working out the number of **vertices** (corners) and edges for a 3D shape.

**You will need** some modelling clay and cocktail sticks. Carefully push the sticks into small balls of modelling clay and join them to make frames for these 3D shapes.

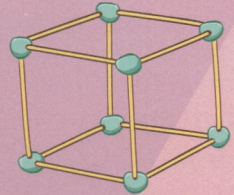 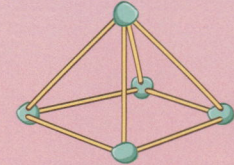 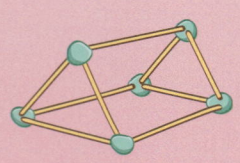

Each clay ball is a vertex; each cocktail stick is an edge.

Complete the table after you have made your models.

| Shape | Number of of faces | Numbers of of edges | Number of vertices |
|---|---|---|---|
| cube | 6 | | |
| square-based pyramid | 5 | | |
| triangular prism | 5 | | |

For each shape work out:

number of faces + number of vertices

number of edges + 2

What do you notice?

## Pyramid poem

Egypt is the place to be
To see a shape that is 3D.
It's huge compared to any kid,
The Pharaoh's giant pyramid.

## FACT
The Great Pyramid at Giza in Egypt is one of the Seven Wonders of the World. It was built over 4,500 years ago!

## FIND OUT
Find out the number of faces on a dodecahedron. What shape are its faces?

30

**3** Milo has bought some sweets for Nina. Dotty shows him how to make a gift box to put them in.

Try making one yourself.

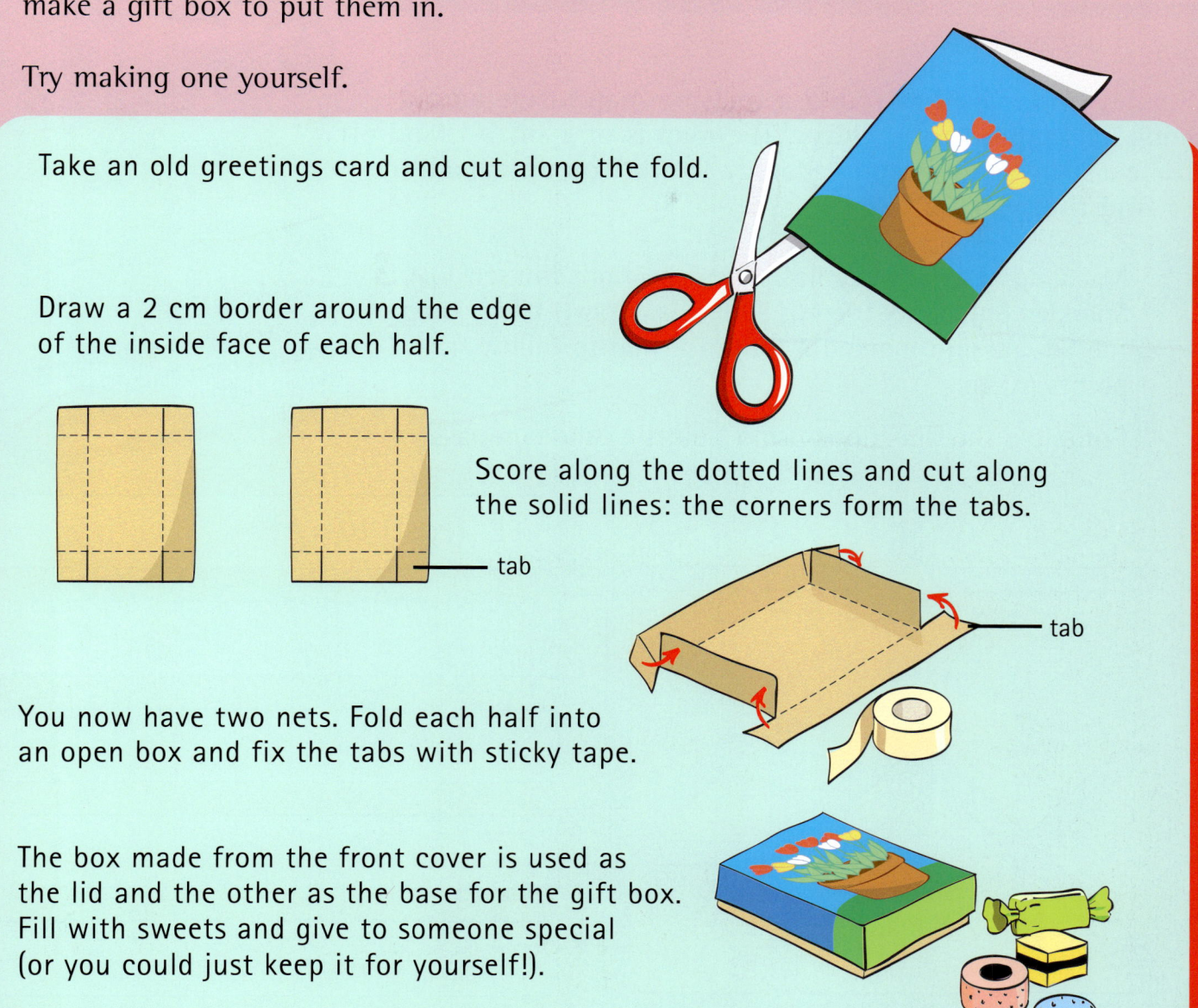

Take an old greetings card and cut along the fold.

Draw a 2 cm border around the edge of the inside face of each half.

tab

Score along the dotted lines and cut along the solid lines: the corners form the tabs.

tab

You now have two nets. Fold each half into an open box and fix the tabs with sticky tape.

The box made from the front cover is used as the lid and the other as the base for the gift box. Fill with sweets and give to someone special (or you could just keep it for yourself!).

**4** Look around your home and outside for 3D shapes used in everyday life. List your objects in the table.

| cube | sphere | cylinder | cuboid | others (pyramids, prisms, cones) |
|------|--------|----------|--------|----------------------------------|
|      |        |          |        |                                  |

# Position and direction

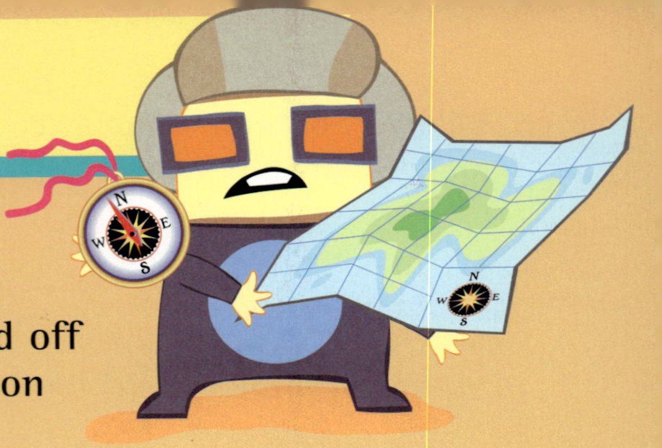

Stanley Spironaut has found a treasure map inside an old book belonging to the Elders. The map is of a small island off the coast of Spark Island. Stanley sets off on an expedition to find the treasure.

**1** Not long after Stanley has set off he finds himself lost in Sparkley Square. A friendly Elder has drawn him a map of the Square and marked a route for him to follow from points Ⓐ to Ⓖ.

Complete the directions using points of the compass.

Sparkley Square

START HERE

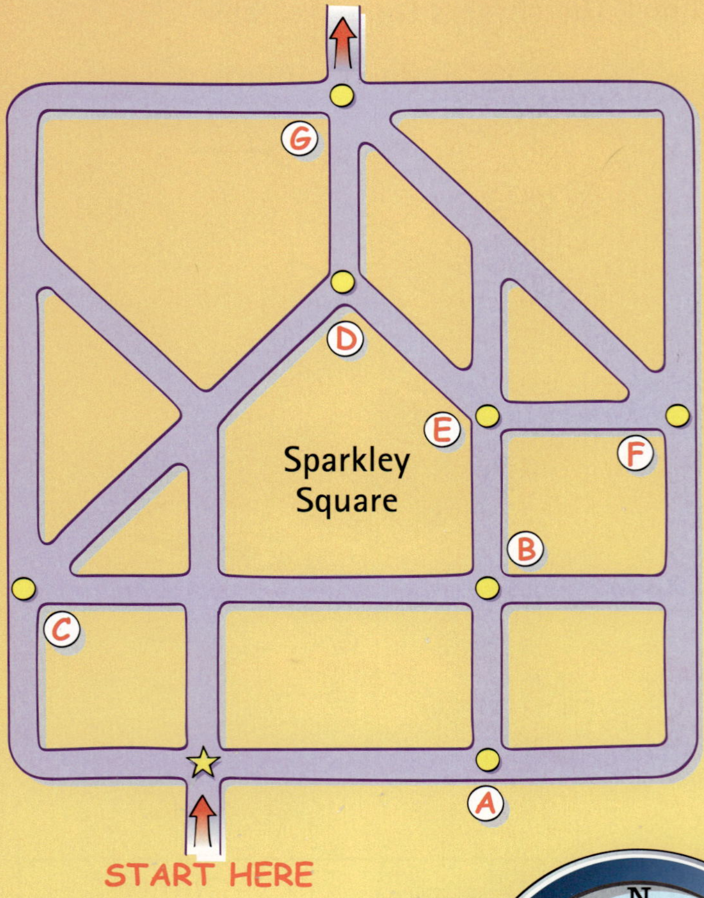

E (east) to Ⓐ

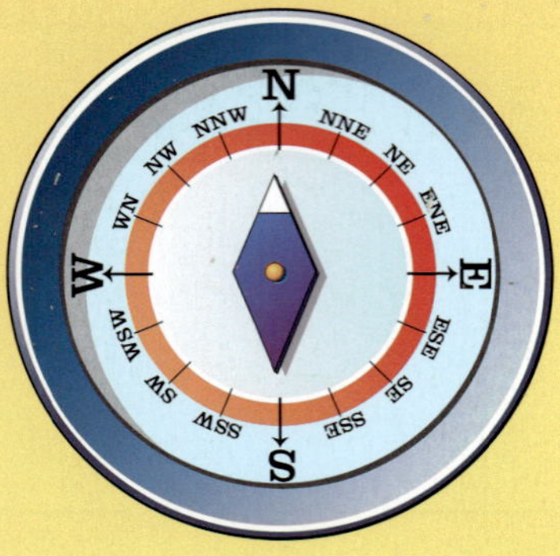

**2**    Now Stanley is ready to follow the treasure map.

**(a)**    Here is Stanley's map.

(i)   What is at (43, 24)?

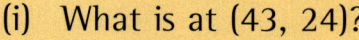

(ii)   What is at (46, 25)?

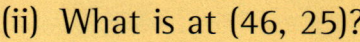

(iii) What is at (47, 28)?

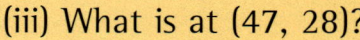

(iv) What is at (42, 29)?

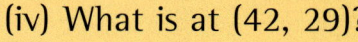

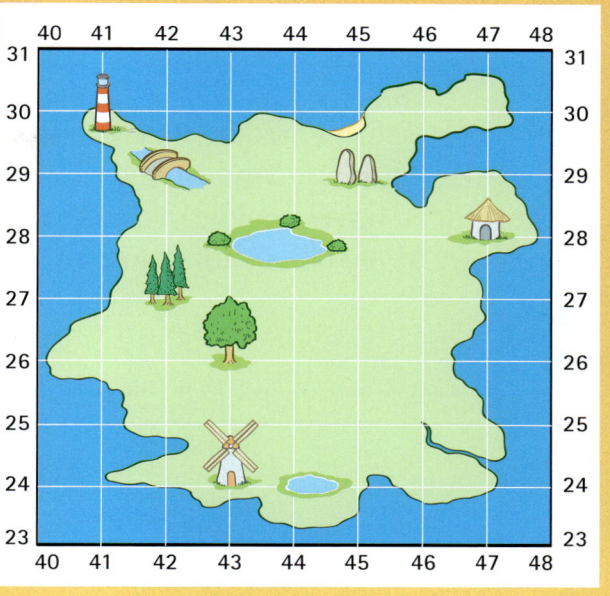

**(b)**    Draw lines to join the four features to make a quadrilateral. Now draw in the diagonals. The treasure is to be found at the point where the diagonals cross.

What are the coordinates of this point?

**3**    Plot these points on the grid to make a shape.

Use an orange pen to plot and join these points:

**(5,0)**   **(3,3)**   **(0,6)**   **(10,6)**

**(7,3)**   **(5,0)**

Use a green pen to plot and join these points:

**(3,3)**   **(7,3)**   **(5,12)**   **(3,3)**

Use a purple pen to plot and join these points:

**(3,3)**   **(1,9)**   **(7,3)**   **(8,1)**

**(5,2)**   **(2,1)**   **(3,3)**   **(9,9)**

**(7,3)**

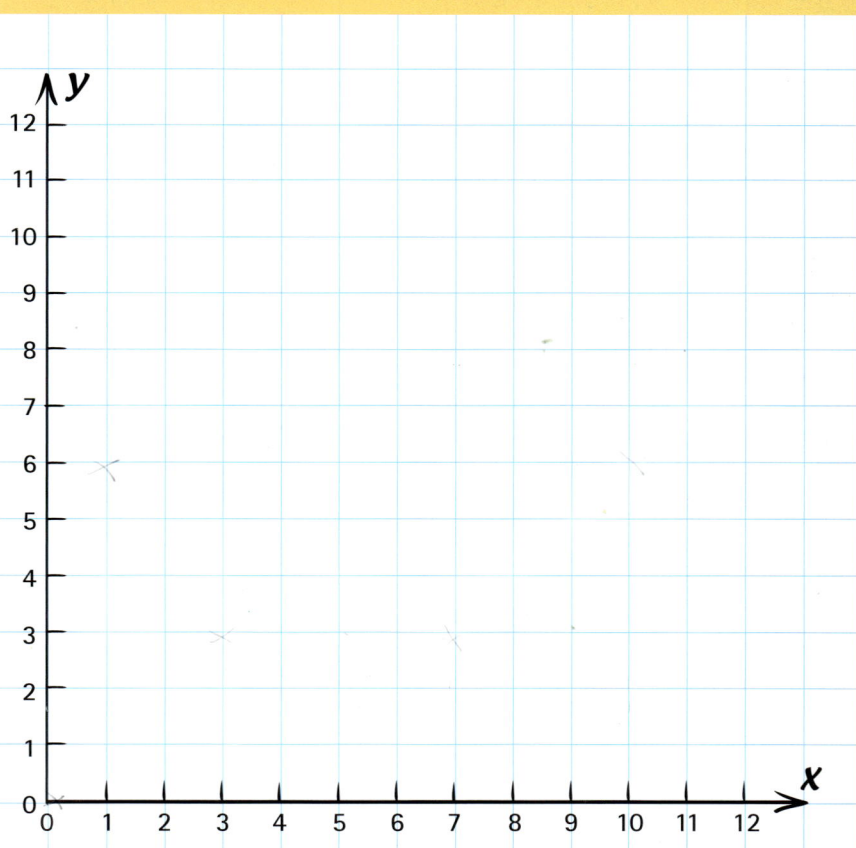

# Perimeter and area

The Xybok are causing havoc on the plains by trampling all over the Elders' crops in search of raspberries and gooseberries. The Elders have decided to divide the fields up into different areas to give the Xybok their own places to graze.

**1**    Here is the Elders' plan for one of the fields.

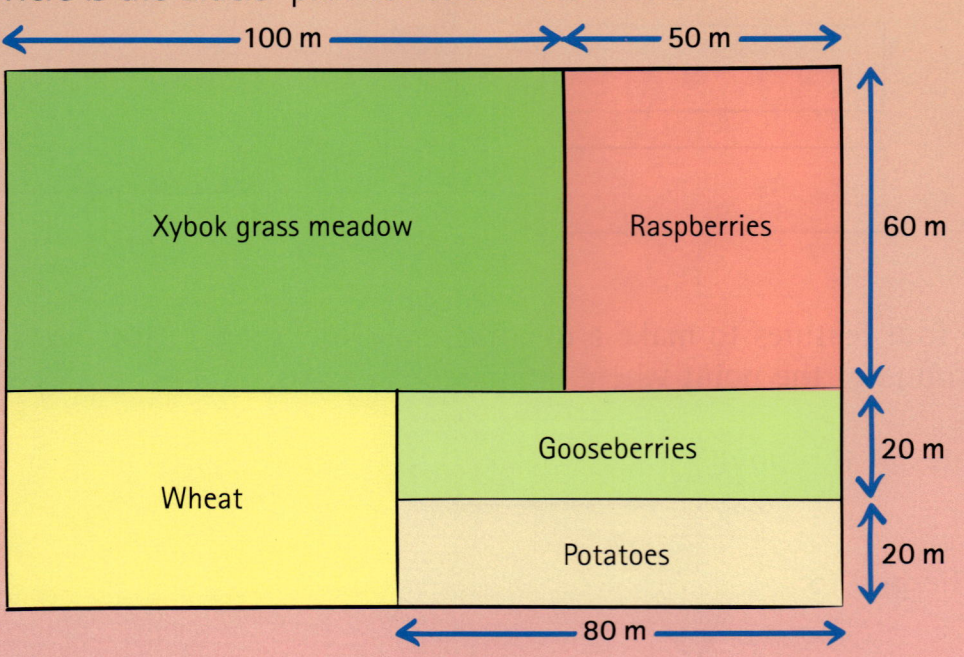

**REMINDER**

The **area** of a rectangle = length x width.

The **perimeter** is the distance around a shape.

Write down the length and width of each section and calculate its area.

| | | | | | | | |
|---|---|---|---|---|---|---|---|
| Meadow | 100 | m | x | 60 | m | = | 6000 | m² |
| Raspberries | | m | x | | m | = | | m² |
| Gooseberries | | m | x | | m | = | | m² |
| Potatoes | | m | x | | m | = | | m² |
| Wheat | | m | x | | m | = | | m²  + |

Total area = [ ] m²

**Zeb's fact file**

The area of the Earth's surface covered by the sea is about 360 000 000 km².

**2**    Three 1 cm squares can be used to make different shapes.
Each shape will have the same area and perimeter.

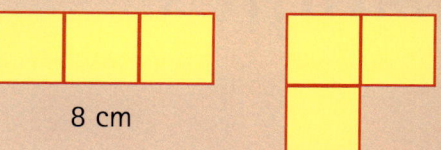

8 cm

(a)    Four squares can also be used to make different shapes all with
the same area, but not all have the same perimeter. Draw your shapes
on the grid below and work out the perimeter of each.

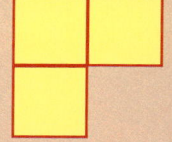

8 cm

(i)   Which one has the shortest perimeter?

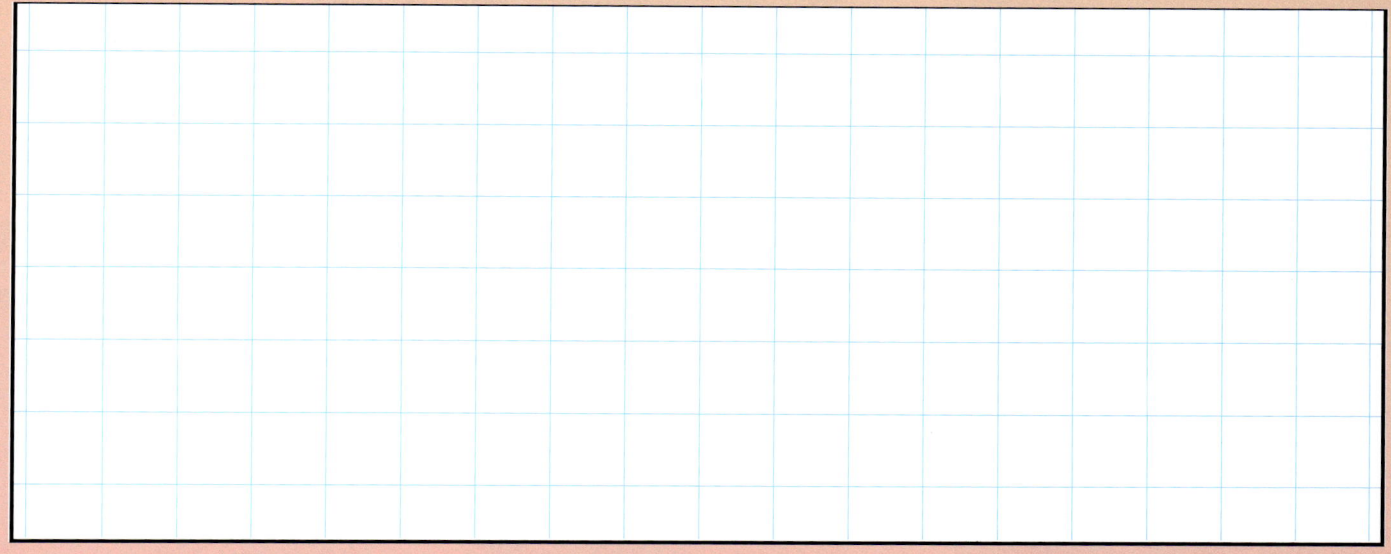

(b)    Now try using 5 squares instead of 4. What has the shortest perimeter?

**3**    The perimeter of a regular polygon can be found by measuring the length of
one side and then multiplying it by the number of sides of the polygon.

For each polygon below, measure one side accurately using a ruler.
Multiply by the number of sides and write the perimeter in the box.

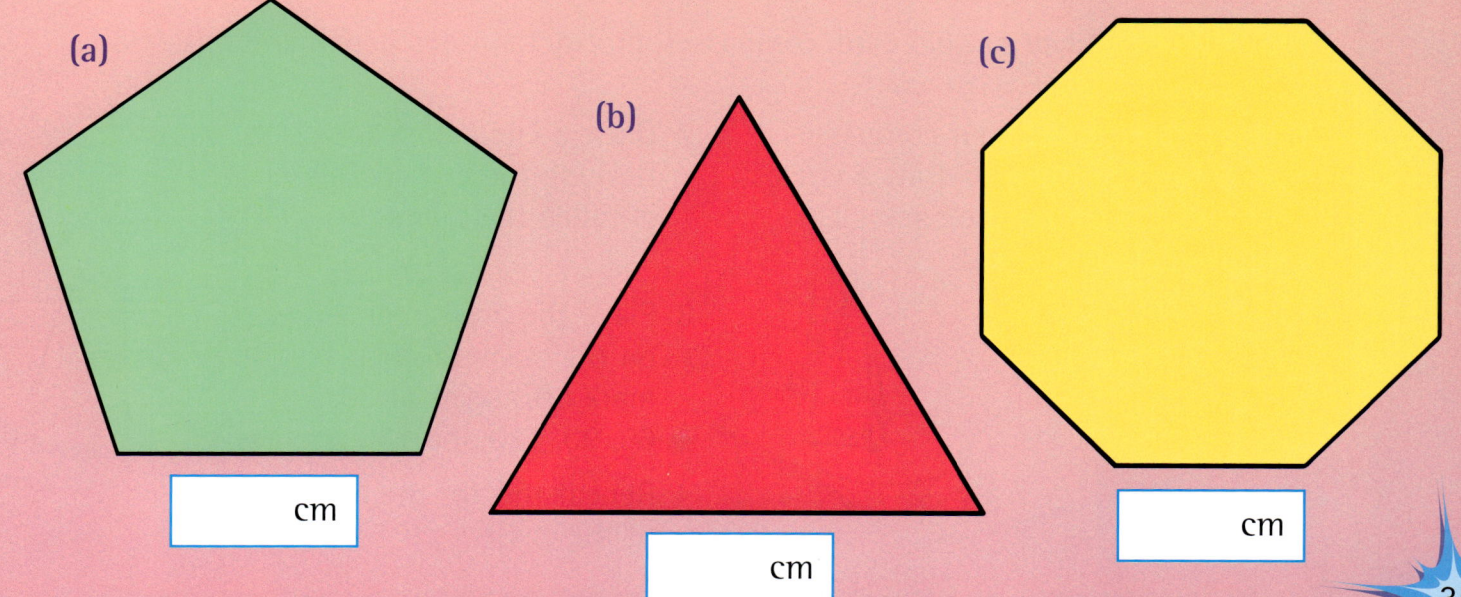

(a)

(b)

(c)

cm

cm

cm

# Angles

**1** The Crombies are busy redesigning their study to make it more trendy and they have bought a new rug. The design they have chosen is shown below.

Look at the design and notice how many different angles there are.
There are eleven acute angles. Put the letter a in each acute angle you find.
There are five obtuse angles. Put the letter o inside each one.
There are six right angles. Put the letter r inside each one.
Finally, there is one reflex angle. Mark it with the letter x.

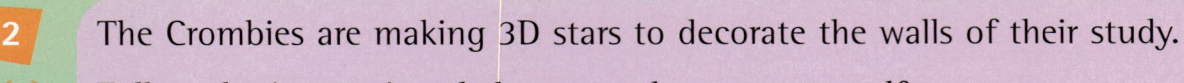

**REMINDER**

The three angles in a triangle always add up to 180 degrees.

An acute angle is smaller than a right angle (90 degrees).

An obtuse angle is more than 90 but less than 180 degrees.

A **reflex angle** is greater than 180 degrees.

**2**

**(a)** The Crombies are making 3D stars to decorate the walls of their study.

Follow the instructions below to make some yourself.

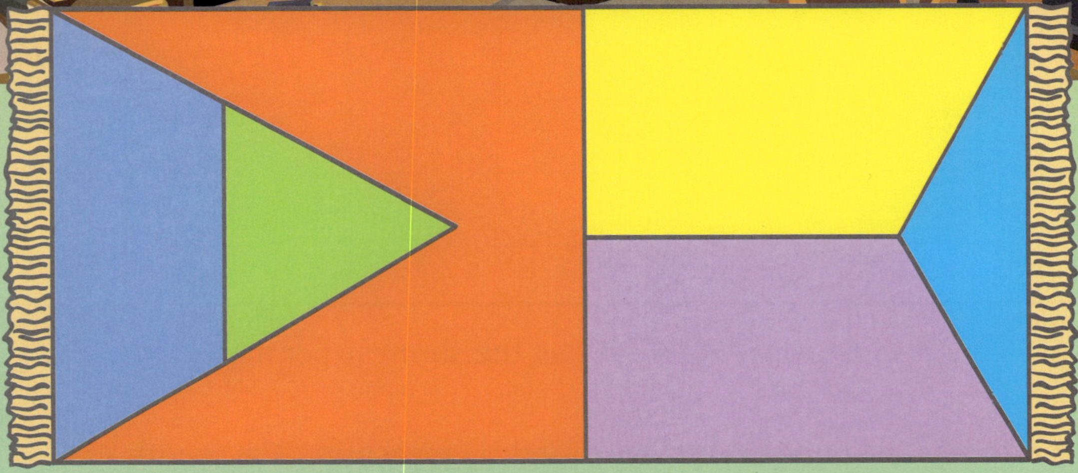

**You will need** silver or gold card, compasses, protractor, ruler, pencil and scissors.

1 Use a ruler to set your compasses to 6 cm. Use them to draw a circle of radius 6 cm on the back (dull side) of the card.

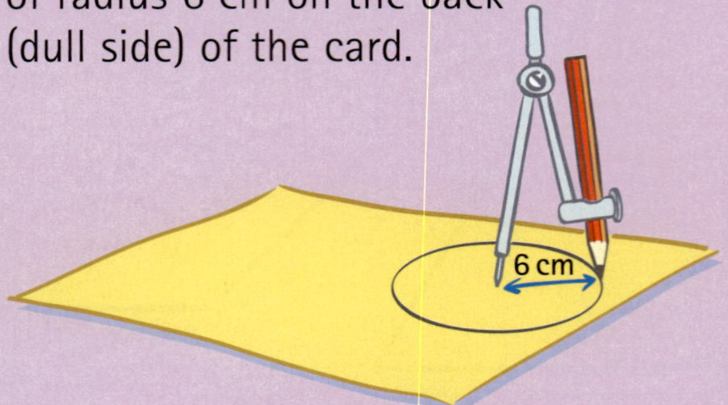

2 Draw a line across the circle through the centre. This is called the **diameter**.

3 Place the protractor on the diameter and mark off angles at 30, 60, 90, 120 and 150 degrees.

4 Repeat this for the other half of the circle.

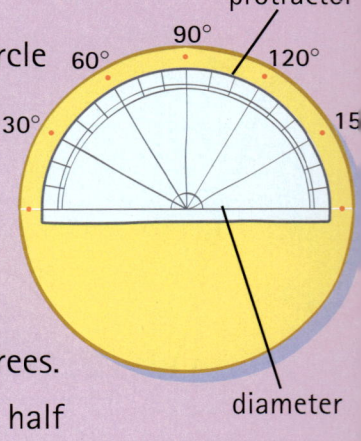

**3** On the squared grid draw the following shapes:
- a triangle with three acute angles
- a quadrilateral with two obtuse angles
- a pentagon with two right angles.

**FIND OUT**
You probably already know that there are 360 degrees in a circle. Can you find out which ancient civilization is thought to have come up with the idea of 360 degrees in a circle.

What do you call a pretty angle?

A cute angle!

**5** Join all the points to the centre.

**6** Now mark the points and join them as shown in the diagram.

30 cm

30 cm

**7** Cut out your star. Then score along the solid lines on the dull side and along the dotted lines on the metallic side.

score here on the dull side

score here on the metallic side

**8** Fold along the creases to create the 3D effect.

You can make different stars by following the same instructions but using different angles. In Step 3 try 45, 90, 135° or 36, 72, 108, 144°.

37

# Symmetry and transformations

**1** Strat is trying on some trendy new T-shirts and is admiring his **reflection** in the mirror. Which of these is his reflection?

Use a mirror to check if you're not sure.

**A mirror key**
Using a mirror is the key To finding lines of symmetry!

A

B

C

D

## Zeb's fact file

You might think your body is symmetrical down the middle. It isn't — one side is not an exact reflection of the other.

**2** The Malvos have been stealing kaleidoscopes from the Elders because they think they are filled with millions of jewels. What they haven't realised is that a kaleidoscope only contains a few worthless beads which are reflected several times in mirrors.

Try making this kaleidoscope but make sure you hide it from the Malvos!

**You will need** 3 pieces of thick mirror card each measuring 3 cm by 15 cm, black card, sticky tape, baking parchment, cling film and tiny bugle beads or sequins.

Tape the three pieces of mirror card together to form a triangular prism.

Cut two triangles from pieces of black card to form the ends of the prism. Cut a 1 cm diameter hole in each one then tape to complete the prism.

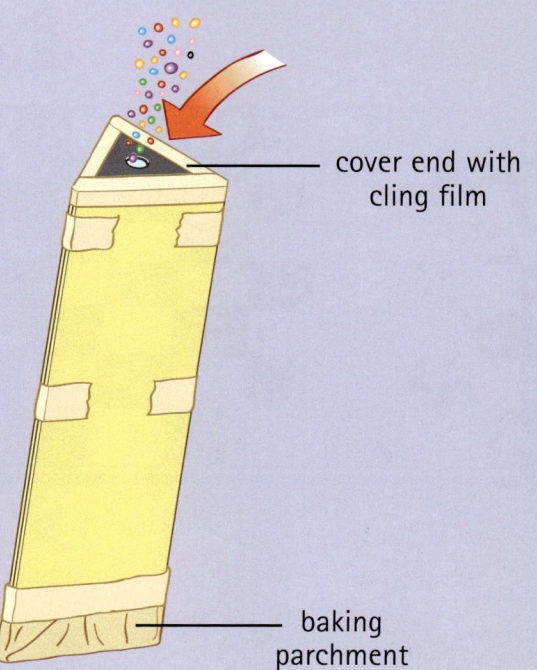

cover end with cling film

Cover and fix one end with baking parchment. Pour a few beads or sequins into the prism from the other end. Seal this end with cling film.

Hold your kaleidoscope up to the light to see the pattern formed. Shake it and look at the new pattern you have created.

baking parchment

**3** Try some more symmetrical patterns.

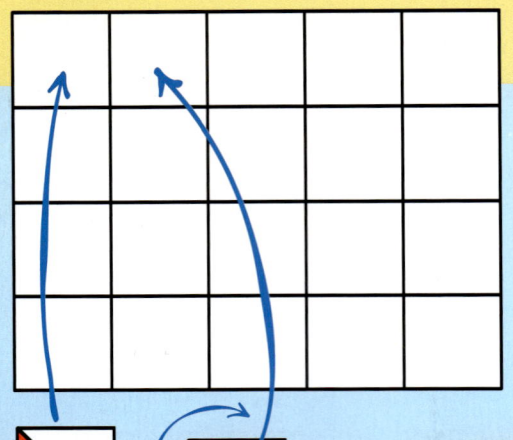

**You will need** a piece of paper divided into 20 squares. In the first square draw a simple coloured design.

In the next square draw your design again but this time rotated through 90 degrees (one quarter turn) clockwise.

Keep rotating your design 90 degrees clockwise each time to continue the pattern.

Have another go but this time try a more complicated design.

draw your design in the first square

rotate it through 90° clockwise and draw in the second square

**4** The Malvos have been playing chess. Vulp has challenged Vole to move the Queen from A to B.

Help Vole to put the instructions on the right in the correct order to complete the challenge.

2 left    5 up

2 right    4 up

3 right    2 up

4 right    4 down

**5** Complete these reflections in the dotted mirror lines to make four mathematical words.

Here's one to help you.

## Find out

Some flags have lines of symmetry.

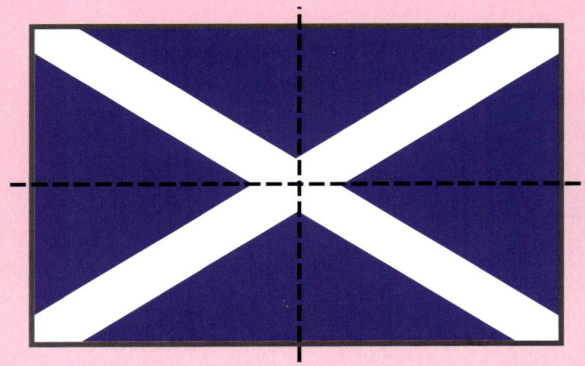
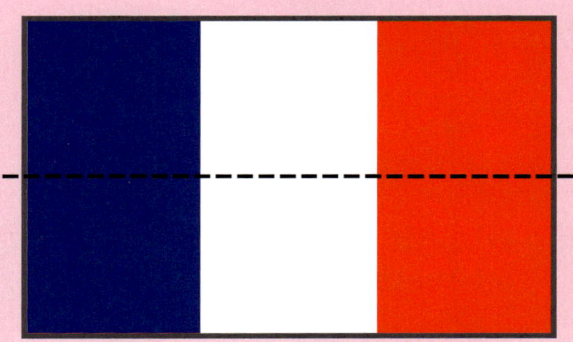

Find out how many lines of symmetry these countries' flags have:

Switzerland     Poland     USA

# Units and measures
## (length, mass, capacity and time)

Many products have a mass, length or capacity marked on their packaging. Masses are given in grams (g) or kilograms (kg), for example, on packets of cereal. Items such as kitchen foil give a length in metres (m) and a width in millimetres (mm) or centimetres (cm). Liquids such as shampoo or fizzy drinks are in containers marked in millilitres (ml) or litres (l).

**1** Look around your home for labels on tins, bottles and packets. Record your findings in a table, listing the items in order of size.

350g

box of cornflakes

| Mass (g, kg) | | Length (mm, cm, m) | | Capacity (ml, l) | |
|---|---|---|---|---|---|
| Item | Quantity | Item | Quantity | Item | Quantity |
| | | | | | |
| | | | | | |
| | | | | | |
| | | | | | |

**2** The Phliplids are planning a visit to the Elders' Museum of Sparkopolis Life on their day off. Here are the museum opening times.

| May 1st – September 30th | October 1st – April 30th |
|---|---|
| Monday – Saturday 8:30 am – 7:45 pm | Monday – Friday 9:00 am – 5:00 pm |
| Sunday 9:00 am – 4:30 pm | Saturday 10:00 am – 4:30 pm |

(i) What time does the Museum open on **Tuesday 5th November?**

(ii) In which months can you only visit the Museum for 6 days each week?

(iii) The Phliplids plan to visit the Museum on **Saturday 2nd March.**

How long is it open for on this day?

**3** Zeb has discovered that every fourth year in our calendar is a 'leap year'. Here is his quick way of remembering how to work out when they occur: if it is a leap year the last two digits of the year can be divided exactly by four.

**REMINDER**
If the last two digits are 00, then it is only a leap year if the four digits are divisible by 400, e.g. 2000 was a leap year, but 2100 is not.

(i) How many leap years were there between 1981 and 1998?

(ii) When are the next three leap years?

(iii) How many actual birthdays would someone born on the 29th of February 1972 have had up until 2003?

**4** Milo thinks his watch is not working properly. So Zeb has suggested they make a minute timer.

Try making one yourself:

**You will need** a 1 litre plastic bottle complete with cap, and a 5 cm length of drinking straw.

1 Ask an adult to pierce a hole in the bottle cap using a skewer. The hole should be the same size as the drinking straw. Pierce another hole in the base of the bottle.

2 Push the straw a short way into the cap. Fill the bottle with water (keeping a finger on the hole in the base!) then screw on the cap and invert the bottle.

3 For exactly one minute collect the water that runs out.

4 Keep the collected water, but empty the remaining water in the bottle. Then pour the collected water into the emptied bottle and invert it, covering both holes to stop the water running out. Ask someone to help you mark the level.

5 You can now use this as a minute timer. Collect the water after each use and pour it back into the bottle.

**5** (a) Estimate the size of this angle in degrees.
Write it down.

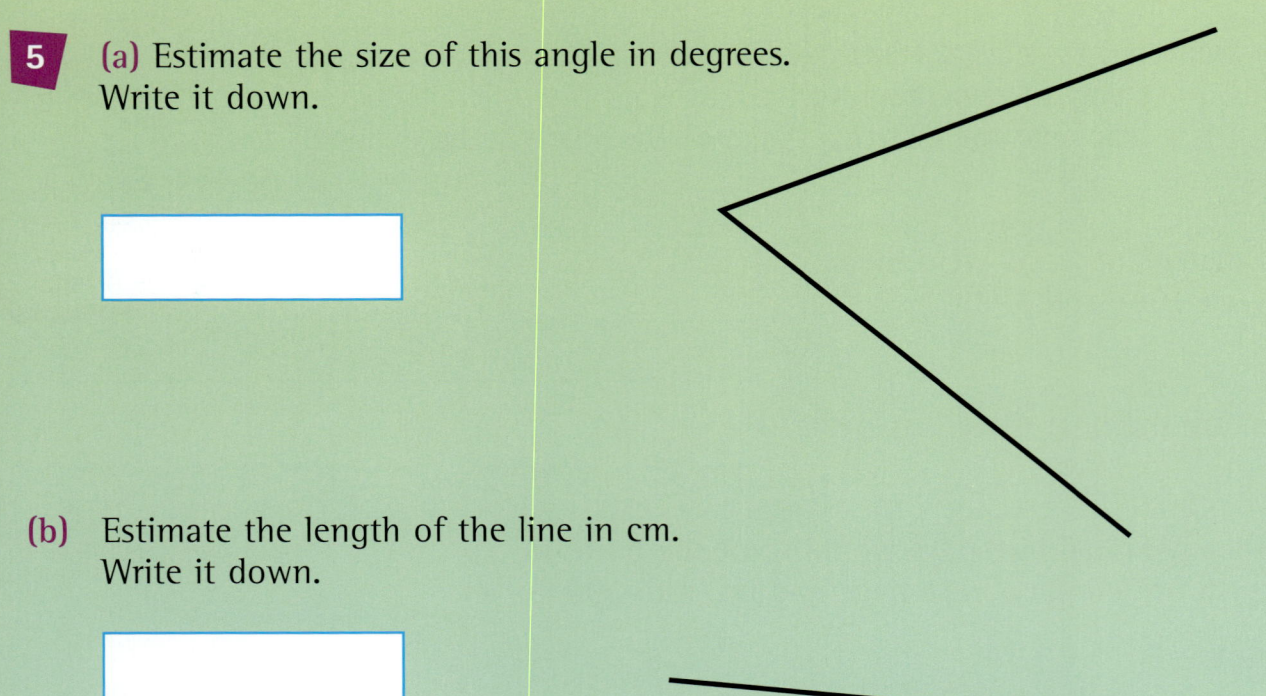

[   ]

(b) Estimate the length of the line in cm.
Write it down.

[   ]

(c) Now measure the angle with a protractor and the line with a ruler.

Check your answers and find out how close your estimates were.

**6** Find five objects in your home which have a mass of about 100 g.

Weigh each object using kitchen scales and record your results by putting a tick in the correct box.

| Object | Exactly 100 g | Less than 100 g | More than 100 g |
| --- | --- | --- | --- |
|  |  |  |  |
|  |  |  |  |
|  |  |  |  |
|  |  |  |  |
|  |  |  |  |

How close were you?

**7** Draw lines to join the matching quantities.

3 l

3·3 m

3 m

0·3 l

300 ml

3000 ml

330 cm

300 cm

30 cm

300 mm

3 km

3000 m

**FIND OUT**

● How many furlongs are in a mile?

● How many yards are in a chain?

● How many ounces are in a pound?

● How many pints in a gallon?

**Zeb's fact file**

Mount Everest, the highest mountain in the world, is 8853 metres.

Roger Bannister was the first man to break the four minute mile.
He ran a time of 3 minutes 59.4 seconds.

# Glossary

| | |
|---|---|
| **acute angle** | an angle less than one quarter turn (90 degrees) |
| **area** | the amount of surface a shape covers |
| **congruent** | identical in size and shape |
| **denominator** | the number on the bottom of a fraction |
| **equilateral triangle** | a triangle with three equal sides and three equal angles (each 60 degrees) |
| **equivalent** | having the same value |
| **factor** | a number which divides exactly into another |
| **heptagon** | a 2D shape with seven sides |
| **hexagon** | a 2D shape with six sides |
| **improper** | a fraction in which the numerator is bigger than the denominator |
| **integer** | a whole number |
| **inverse** | the opposite operation |
| **isosceles triangle** | a triangle with two equal sides and two equal angles |
| **kite** | a quadrilateral with two pairs of equal adjacent sides |
| **mean** | the average, which is found by adding all values together and then dividing the total by the number of values |
| **median** | the middle value of a set of numbers when listed in order of size |
| **mode** | the most common item or number in a list |
| **multiples** | the answers to a multiplication table |
| **numerator** | the number on the top of a fraction |
| **obtuse angle** | an angle between a quarter (90 degrees) and a half turn (180 degrees) |
| **octagon** | a 2D shape with eight sides |

| | |
|---|---|
| **parallel** | lines which are the same distance apart |
| **parallelogram** | a quadrilateral with two pairs of opposite sides which are equal in length and parallel |
| **pentagon** | a 2D shape with five sides |
| **percentage** | the number of parts in every one hundred |
| **perimeter** | the distance around a flat shape |
| **perpendicular** | at right angles |
| **polygon** | a 2D shape with straight sides |
| **prime number** | a number that can only be divided by one and itself |
| **probability** | a measure of how likely it is for something to happen |
| **product** | the result when two numbers are multiplied |
| **quadrilateral** | a 2D shape with four sides |
| **quotient** | the answer when one number is divided by another |
| **reflection** | the mirror image of a shape |
| **reflex angle** | an angle greater than a half turn (180 degrees) |
| **rhombus** | a quadrilateral with four equal sides, opposite pairs of sides are parallel and opposite angles are equal |
| **rotation** | the direction and angle of a turn |
| **scalene triangle** | a triangle with three unequal angles and unequal sides |
| **sequence** | a list of numbers which are linked by a rule (sometimes called a number chain) |
| **translation** | sliding up/down and/or left/right |
| **trapezium** | a quadrilateral with only one pair of parallel sides |
| **vertex** | a corner of a 2D or 3D shape (vertices is plural of vertex) |
| **volume** | the amount of space filled by a 3D object |

## Answers

### Numbers and the number system

1  101, 181, 619, 689, 888, 808, 906, 916, 986

2  24 Hours in a Day, 21 Days in February in a Leap Year, 11 Players in a Football Team, 7 Wonders of the World

3  7 VII, 16 XVI, 34 XXXIV, 67 LXVII, 101 CI, 630 DCXXX, 1254 MCCLIV

4  -200, -41, -40, -16, -13, -3, -1, 0, 1 (spells out SPIRONAUT)

5  JETPACK
   **Find out** brace – 2; score – 20; dozen – 12; gross - 144

### Calculations

1  74, 60, 80; Xavi scored most

2  (a) 941 + 743 (or 943 + 741) = 1684  (b) 149 + 347 (or 147 + 349) = 496  (c) 94 + 73 + 41 = 208 (others possible)

3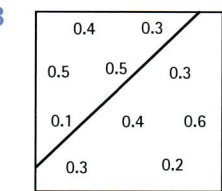

4  50 + 2 = 52 then 52 x 5 = 260 then 260 + 9 - 6 = 263

5  (a) 1 + 2 = 3; 2 + 3 = 5; 1 + 2 + 3 = 6; 3 + 4 = 7; 4 + 5 = 9; 1 + 2 + 3 + 4 = 10; 5 + 6 = 11; 3 + 4 + 5 = 12; 6 + 7 = 13; 2 + 3 + 4 + 5 = 14; 8 + 9 = 17; 5 + 6 + 7 = 18; 9 + 10 = 19

   (b) 1, 2, 4, 8, 16 can't be done. They make a sequence formed by doubling.

6

| 16 | 3  | 2  | 13 |
|----|----|----|----|
| 5  | 10 | 11 | 8  |
| 9  | 6  | 7  | 12 |
| 4  | 15 | 14 | 1  |

   **Numbers to words**  1 hedgehog  2 shoes  3 solids

7  (a) £4.80  (b) £12.80

### Properties of numbers and sequences

1  9, 18, 45, 63, 90

2  15

3  (a) 5 + 7 = 12; 2 + 23 = 25; 13 + 3 (or 5 + 11) = 16; 2 + 2 + 17 = 21

   (b) 3 x 5 = 15; 5 x 11 = 55; 2 x 13 = 26; 2 x 3 x 5 = 30

4  2, 4, 6, 12, 24

5  (a) 26  (b) 23  (c) 5

6

| 5  | 6  | 30 |
|----|----|----|
| 9  | 16 | 36 |
| 21 | 14 | 28 |

7  (a) 11  (b) number of pegs = number of shirts + 1

### Fractions, decimals and percentages

1

| $\frac{1}{2}$ | $\frac{4}{12}$ | $\frac{1}{3}$ | $\frac{9}{24}$ | $\frac{3}{8}$ | $\frac{10}{16}$ | $\frac{5}{8}$ | $\frac{10}{80}$ |
|---|---|---|---|---|---|---|---|
| $\frac{4}{2}$ | | | | | | | $\frac{8}{1}$ |
| $\frac{5}{3}$ | | | | | | | $\frac{6}{8}$ |
| $\frac{9}{15}$ | | | | | | | $\frac{3}{4}$ |
| $\frac{2}{3}$ | | | | | | | $\frac{8}{10}$ |
| $\frac{8}{12}$ | $\frac{2}{5}$ | $\frac{4}{10}$ | $\frac{1}{4}$ | $\frac{12}{3}$ | $\frac{5}{1}$ | $\frac{4}{20}$ | $\frac{4}{5}$ |

2  Blackspark Road

3  (a) 21, 21·2; 25, 24·8; 21, 20·9; 18, 18·1; 17, 17·5
   (b) Strat 1st, Nina 2nd, Zeb 3rd
   (c) 7·31 seconds

4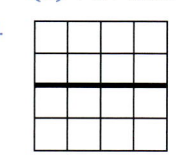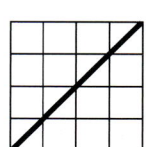
   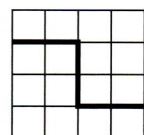 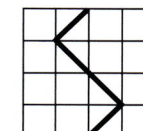  others possible

5  (a) shade 20 pieces; shade 12 pieces  (b) $\frac{1}{3}$  (c) $\frac{1}{5}$

### Ratio and proportion

1  butter: 100 g  flour: 150 g

2  (a) 600 ml lemonade  (b) 1000 ml or 1 litre of Orange Sparkle  (c) 125 ml syrup and 875 ml milk

3  6 yellow; 8 green; 3 pink; 7 blue

4  15:10 and 3:2; 16:16 and 1:1; 5:10 and 1:2; 8:4 and 2:1; 4:16 and 1:4

## Handling data

3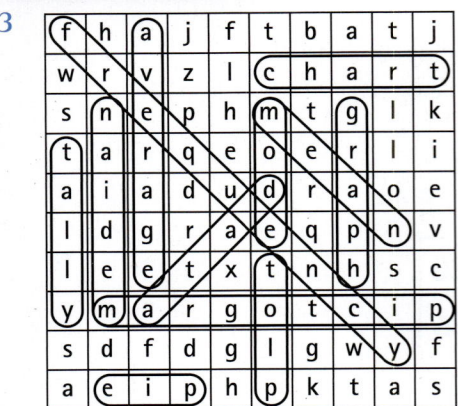

5 (a) 6·9 kg  (b) 1·15 kg

6 (a) Raspberry  (b) 25  (c) 5

7 (a) Brazil  (b) 281 million  (c) France and Spain
(d) 3  (e) naira

## Probability

1 (a) 2 and 12  (b) 3  (c) $\frac{3}{36} = \frac{1}{12}$

2 Take-a-chance:  E  The probability of getting 3 is
$\frac{1}{2}$ and only $\frac{1}{4}$ for 1 or 2. Or, the probability of
landing on 3 is the same as that for landing on 1
for spinners A to D.

## 2D shapes

1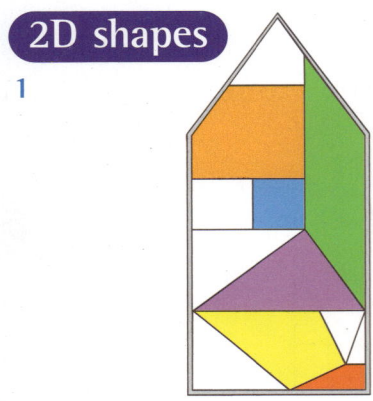

**What am I?**  a kite

## 3D shapes

1 fourth solid - cylinder (has curved face)

2 cube 12, 8; pyramid 8, 5; prism 9, 6; faces + vertices
= edges + 2

**Find out**  12 faces; each face is a regular pentagon

## Position and direction

1 E to (A), N to (B), W to (C), NE to (D), SE to (E),
E to (F), NW to (G)

2 (a) (i) windmill (ii) river source (iii) hut (iv) bridge
(b) (45, 26)

3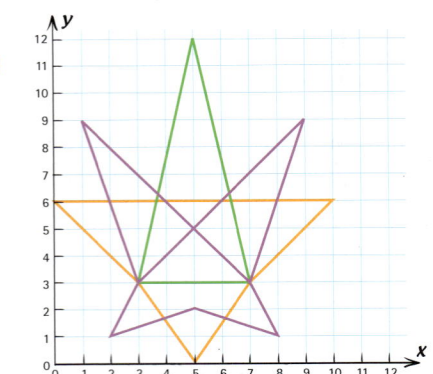

## Perimeter and area

1 100 x 60 = 6000; 50 x 60 = 3000; 80 x 20 = 1600;
80 x 20 = 1600; 70 x 40 = 2800; Total area 15000

2 (a) 8 cm  (b) 10 cm

3 (a) 4 cm, 20 cm  (b) 6·5 cm, 19·5 cm
(c) 2·5 cm, 20 cm

## Angles

1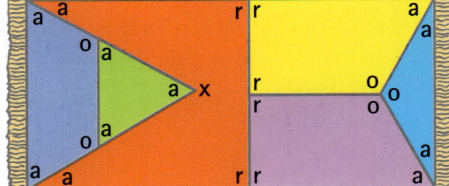

3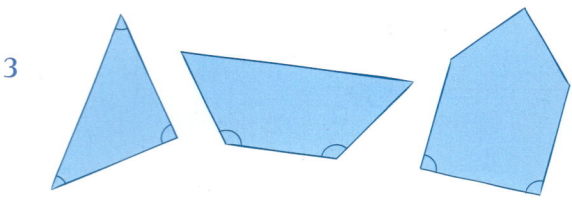

**Find out**  Ancient Babylonians

## Symmetry and transformations

1 D

4 3 right 2 up; 2 left 5 up; 4 right 4 down;
2 right 4 up, or reverse of these

5 TWO, DIVIDE, CUBE, DECIMAL

**Find out**  Switzerland – 4; Poland – 1; USA - 0

## Units and measures

2 (i) 9:00 am (ii) October–April (iii) 6 and a half hours

3 (i) 4 (ii) 2004, 2008, 2012  (iii) 7

5 (a) 60 degrees  (b) 8 cm

7 300 ml and 0·3 l; 3000 ml and 3 l; 3.3 m and
330 cm; 3 m and 300 cm; 3 km and 3000 m;
30 cm and 300 mm

**Find out**  8 furlongs in a mile, 22 yards in a chain, 16
ounces in a pound, 8 pints in a gallon